YOUR CAREER IN BUSINESS

Walter Hoving

TIFFANY & CO.
NEW YORK

Second Printing, December 1978
Copyright © Walter Hoving 1977
Library of Congress Catalogue Card Number: 77-75738
Printed in the United States of America

Contents

YOUR CAREER
IN
BUSINESS

They're Looking for Jobs

My secretary came in to tell me that young Mr. Garver had arrived for his appointment.

"Who is Mr. Garver?" I asked.

"He's the young man whose father wrote—the letter is on top of your papers."

"Oh, yes," and I re-read the letter.

"My object in writing you," the letter stated, "is to inquire about the possibility of a position for my son. He has just finished college and is now twenty-two. He is a clean-cut young man, six feet two, ambitious and willing to work. I shall greatly appreciate your giving him an interview, etc."

This letter is not vastly different from many I receive every month. It bears upon the problem of the young person who has finished school, and is trying to find a job.

"He's right on time," I remarked.

"They always are," my secretary replied, "when they are looking for a position."

Young Mr. Garver sat down beside my desk.

"So you want to go into business," I began.

"Yes, I do, indeed," he answered.

"What kind of business do you think you would like to go into?"

"Why, I don't know; I just want to go into business."

"But what kind of businessman do you want to be? Do you believe that you would make a salesman or an accountant or a journalist, or do you think you have aptitudes for other occupations?"

"I haven't thought about that," he answered.

"Have you tried to figure out whether you have any business ability of anykind?"

"No," he admitted, "I don't believe I have."

"Have you attempted to find out whether you have any other abilities—analyzed yourself in any way?"

"Well, only in a very general way," he replied.

"Do you think, for example, you would make an executive?"

His face lit up. "Yes," he answered promptly. "I would like to be an executive."

"Well, now," I said, "if you have decided that, have you ever done anything that would indicate that you have, at least in embryo, the qualities of an executive? Have you ever tried to run anything, to manage anything?"

"I don't understand."

"I mean this—after all, an executive must manage other people. Have you ever managed other people, even in a small way, such as running a fraternity dance or managing a football team? Have you done any kind of group managing, either of boys or girls?"

"No," he acknowledged after a little pause, "I never have."

"Do you think, then," I persisted, "that you are lacking in this quality?

"Well," he said, "perhaps I am—I don't know."

"Look here, Garver," I finally said, "you haven't really tried very hard to find out what kind of person you are, have you? Or in what way you can be useful to those who might employ you? You don't know very much about yourself, do you, from this point of view?"

"No," he said frankly, "I guess I don't."

"Let me give you a bit of advice, then. You are trying to sell yourself to me for a job of some kind, aren't you? To do that you must know something about your product, which in this case happens to be you. Suppose you came in here and tried to sell me an automobile, and I asked you similar questions—not about yourself, but about the car. If I asked you the number of cylinders, the wheel base, the kind of body, or whether the chassis is strong enough to take a long trip, you would be expected to answer those questions intelligently, wouldn't you?"

He nodded.

"But," I continued, "you are not selling cars this time; you are selling yourself. And you are unable to tell me about the product. After all, I am buying what you can do, and that depends on your abilities, your interests, your education, your training. Suppose you think it over for a few weeks and then come back and we'll have another chat."

Here was a young man who had reached the age of twenty-two without giving any intelligent thought to the future. Like tens of thousands of others, his plans were vague and indefinite. He would go into business, he decided, since business was a way of making a living. But all that was ahead of him, a problem to tackle after graduation. In the meantime, there was no use worrying

3

about it; so apparently he dismissed the question and settled down to the enjoyment of his college life and his summer vacations.

This is the attitude of thousands of young men and women who are finishing schools and colleges, and the composite picture is not very pleasant to contemplate. It accounts in part for the vast number of misfits in business, for the wasted abilities, for the middle-aged employees who lament "I always wanted to do that, or to try that, but now it is too late to make a fresh start."

A few weeks after this interview, I received the following letter:

Dear Mr. Hoving:

Since my very interesting and helpful talk with you last month, I have followed your advice and have done a great deal of thinking about the line of business I should go into. During this time, I also made a study of the most important department and chain stores in the city from which I have gained some valuable information about the merchandising business. At the same time, I have talked with other men in other fields, which has enabled me gradually to formulate my plans for the future. If, at the end of a period of experimentation, I should definitely decide to enter the field of merchandising, I sincerely hope that you will allow me to talk with you again.

This was an excellent start. It indicated that young Garver was at least doing some thinking about the type of business he was best suited for; he was beginning to approach his problems objectively and in an orderly way.

Here is an instance of a young woman's approach to this business of earning a living.

4

"I have decided," Miss Ingersoll told me, "to try for a career in merchandising."

"Tell me the steps that led you to this conclusion."

"Well," she hesitated, "I can't say I have any logical reason for deciding to enter such a career, but I would like to try it."

"I see. Well, then, tell me about yourself."

"I was educated at Northwestern University and also at schools and colleges in Paris. My father lived in Paris for a great many years. Three years after I was graduated, I became interested in photography. As a matter of fact, I have done a great deal of photographic work for the government. Although I believe I have a knack for photography, it is only a knack. I don't think I have enough ability to outdistance others in the game. Therefore, I decided not to devote any more time to this field."

"That," I said, "is a very sensible conclusion. I take it, then, that you feel you have a more natural aptitude for merchandising."

"No," she said, "I can't say that I figured that out— but, as I said in the beginning, I should like to try."

Obviously, she did not seem to feel that any natural talent for merchandising was necessary in order to succeed in this field. She did not consider that it was as essential to have an aptitude for merchandising as it was to have an aptitude for photography. One field, she quickly recognized, required special skills; the other field was just business. Anyone, apparently, who was willing to work could handle it satisfactorily, she thought.

On the other hand, a young man of my acquaintance had spent several of his summers working, checking barrel supplies in a chemical plant, keeping track of farm labor on a large wheat farm in Minnesota, and running a camp for delinquent boys. In order to run this camp efficiently, he had to start arranging his organization in April. He had to purchase all supplies and plan his counselors' duties in order to be ready for the boys when they arrived. By the end of the summer he had grown tremendously. He knew how to organize and run things; he knew how to discipline a group of boys; he knew how to plan and make both ends meet.

Unfortunately, in most cases these important questions of planning and preparing for the future do not receive much consideration, neither by undergraduates themselves, nor by many educators and parents. And yet, these are the most important questions the individual has to answer. Little practical attention is paid to solving the problem, however, except by the most enlightened educators, and there are thousands upon thousands of young men and women who finish their schooling without having given any thought to the kind of work to which they will devote most of their active hours for the rest of their lives.

They do not know themselves, their capacities, or the way in which these can be used to the best advantage, both to their own satisfaction and advancement, and for the benefit of their prospective employers. They have given no consideration to the various fields of business, their functions, and the skills they require.

They are simply looking for a job. But a job should not be the goal. It is merely the starting post. The more intelligence one puts into that initial choice, the better chance there is of advancing toward a definite goal. Those who follow the nearest path often end nowhere, and those who make too many false starts may never get far from the starting post.

And so they come, young men and young women, willing, for the most part, to work hard but with no very clear understanding of what it is they have to sell and no convictions about what they want to do.

This haphazard approach with no goal in view, this well-intentioned, but aimless, willingness to do anything, this helpless, trusting reliance on someone else to start you in the right direction, are the reasons why so many young people who went into business yesterday are floundering today, no better off than when they started, and why so many who are starting out today "to look for a job" will be floundering tomorrow.

Business Has Many Facets

What is this thing called business where the great majority of people work and on which their livelihoods depend?

Business, in its essence, is the whole process which brings to people the things they need: food, clothing, services, transportation, education, homes, home furnishings, adornments, luxuries, amusements; and anything else people consume.

There are many definitions of business and many interpretations of it, and there is a great deal of general misunderstanding of its methods as well as its functions. But in its broadest sense, business is the generic term for the whole system, for the highly complicated structure, which in an era of specialization provides people with everything they need.

This function, until very recent times, was the province of a host of individual workers, of solitary workmen who produced the articles they sold to individuals. The shoemaker in his little shop made shoes by hand for his customers, but the cost was high, and the people who could afford his product were few. Today shoes are made by mass production, turned out in great quantities, more quickly and, above all, more cheaply than was possible under the old system; consequently they have become available to great numbers of people who could not otherwise afford them. The great advantage, obviously, is that the present system makes it possible for more people to have more goods and services.

Now there are a great many misconceptions held by those who are going into business as to what it is all about, what its possibilities are for them, and what it means as a way of life.

Business is one of the great adventures in modern life. True, business reaches out, with its highly complicated mesh, into every phase of activity. But it isn't stifling enterprise; it is creating opportunities, more varied, more promising than ever before. There is no reason for the sense of discouragement which assails so many people when they first look at the complexity of business. There's every reason to be discouraged if you wander aimlessly into business, satisfied to let someone else size you up and fit you into the first place that seems available.

To sit around, waiting for some businessman to decide for you what you are capable of doing, without bothering to think it out for yourself, is obviously stupid. Yet of the hundreds of thousands of young people who graduate from schools and colleges every year, most of them are inclined to do just that.

First of all, business is divided into various broad classifications. A few of them are manufacturing, distribution, transportation, publishing, insurance, mining, and banking. Each is fundamentally different from the others, and each presents basically different problems.

9

But business is also divided into work activities. Some of them may be listed as follows: designing, making, selling, record-keeping, financing, engineering, research, personnel administration, management, and so forth. All of these work activities are quite different and they require different skills and abilities. They are even more specialized than those under the industry classifications. Engineering skill, for instance is quite different from the skill required in personnel work, financing is unlike advertising, and designing is different from research.

Although selling is of paramount importance in the field of distribution, other work activities are also necessary. The product must be financed while in the process of distribution, record-keeping is important to keep track of expenses and sales, and the activities of advertising and research are required. Engineering is needed to maintain the plant or store and heat and ventilate it. And personnel work must be done in order to have the proper staff to carry on the work.

Thus it can be seen that in every industry many classifications of work activities are necessary. Each of them requires people who have the proper abilities. Some of you have the ability to make things, others to design, still others have the capacity for selling and advertising. A different type of individual has a talent for engineering and another seems to be particularly good at research work. Some people have a leaning toward finance and still others are good at keeping records.

In addition to this, as the industrial classifications are further divided, more facets appear. For instance, manufacturing can be divided into many types. The making of automobiles, furniture, men's clothing, women's ready-to-wear, machinery, airplanes, and carpets, to mention only a few of the many, many thousands of different types of manufacturing. As a matter of fact, it has been estimated that there are about 21,000 different kinds of jobs in business.

The skills necessary in manufacturing automobiles are different from those needed to make clothing. One requires an entirely different type of designing from the other. The manufacturing processes are also as different as day is from night. Advertising, engineering, and financing all vary a great deal from one industry to another. Record-keeping and research, it might be said, are the only two activities that remain essentially the same, although even they vary a great deal.

The functions of management also vary greatly with the type of business involved. A person who can manage one thing may be unsuccessful in managing another. There is a wide difference between sales management and factory management. Management of a bank and management of research are also entirely different. Office management is not the same thing as stage management. Although this seems self-evident, I have seen more mistakes made in the field of management than in any other field.

It is not at all uncommon to see men with a bent for office management doing a sales management job, or men with an aptitude for research management trying to run newspapers or magazines. Indeed, it is hard to find a company in which these mistakes are not often made.

To illustrate some of the many skills in business management, here are some excerpts taken from an executive rating card in a large Eastern company. The purpose is to appraise executives and to determine how well they do their work.

1. Does he organize his work?
2. Does he get things done?
3. Does he distinguish between the important and the unimportant?
4. Is he attentive to details?
5. Does he adapt himself quickly to new situations?
6. Is the level of his performance consistent?
7. Does he show judgement and foresight in requisitioning additional help?
8. Does he work without depending on his superior?
9. Is he observing?
10. Is he prompt in action?
11. Is he effective in teaching and giving criticism?
12. Is he a good disciplinarian?
13. Does he get enthusiastic response through his personality?
14. Has he initiative?
15. Has he imagination?

Here is a set of rating queries for an advertising copy-writer, which indicates some of the different qualities which are necessary for this type of job:

1. Does she express herself well?
2. Is her style sophisticated and smart?
3. Has she creative imagination?
4. Has she fashion sense?
5. Has she showmanship?
6. Are her ideas practical?
7. Is she aggressive enough to get her ideas across to those for whom she writes copy? Or does she let them dominate her?
8. Does she organize her work?
9. Is she tactful in her relationships?

10. Does she follow through?
11. Is the level of her performance consistent?
12. Does she get along well with people?
13. Is she cooperative with other departments.

The following questions are used in rating salespeople in a department store:

1. Does she act as host to the customer?
2. Does she make the customer feel important?
3. Does she show good judgement in difficult situations?
4. Does she analyze the customer's need?
5. Does she present the merchandise well?
6. Does she close a sale quickly?
7. Does she make good suggestions?
8. Does she volunteer merchandise and fashion information?
9. Does she sell and suggest additional merchandise?
10. Does she know the stock well?
11. Is her knowledge expert?
12. Do customers return to her?
13. Does she do any organized follow-up?
14. Is she well groomed?
15. Has she a pleasant expression?
16. Is she alert? Enthusiastic?
17. Does she keep stock orderly and in good condition on her own initiative?
18. Does she show good taste in display?
19. Does she know the store system? Handle it correctly?
20. Does she work quickly? Does she take pressure well?

21. Does she get along well with people? Cooperate?
22. Is she interested in her job?
23. Does she react well to suggestion and criticism?

Now let's get down to brass tacks.

Let us suppose that you are standing looking at a huge wall. And on this wall are 21,000 padlocks hanging on pegs. These locks represent all the different businesses and jobs in the country.

Now suppose you take a key out of your pocket. This key represents you. It is entirely different from any other key. The indentations and the irregularities on your key represent your aptitudes and abilities; to the degree that you differ from your friends, your key would differ from theirs.

The next thing is to try to fit your key into the proper lock on the wall. If you do what most people do—the people I have been describing—you will try one lock after another, more or less at random, trying to find the lock your key fits. This lock would be *your* business, and your place in that business. The thing that happens to most men and women, however, is that they never find the proper lock, and consequently lose much valuable time while they continue to try one job after another.

There are thousands of people selling who should not be doing it, while thousands of others, who might make excellent salesmen, try to be bookkeepers or statisticians, but lack the aptitude for it. Why is this mistake so generally made? Because few people make an intelligent analysis of their own abilities and try to check them against the skills demanded in the jobs they take. And yet

14

it must be obvious that the person who tries to fit into a job which requires abilities which he lacks is only fighting a losing game.

The purpose of this book, therefore, is to help you find your career in business.

The Thing Called Personality

If you have done much thinking about this problem of going into business, it is likely that at one time and another you have looked over the "Want Ads" to learn something about a possible market for your wares. Have you ever noticed how often the advertisements, after listing other qualifications, add the word *attractive?* That doesn't mean that the prospective employer is looking for someone who can qualify for the movies. It means, as a rule, merely that you are expected to be a pleasant person.

Whatever your qualifications may be, they can, on the whole, be tested only in actual employment. It is the impression you make which decides whether you are to have an opportunity to display your qualifications. Suppose you give a quick check-up of the things about you which are apt to influence that first impression.

First of all, of course, there is your *personality.* For our purposes, I am going to use the narrow meaning of the word, illustrated by the expressions: "He has a splendid personality," or "She is a very attractive girl."

Personality may be defined as those qualities and skills which enable one person agreeably to reach others, plus the courage to do so. Let's take a look at the qualities which bear on personality.

Intelligence, of course, is important. Obviously, if you are dull, it will be difficult for you to reach other people.

Humor is an important personal quality, particularly the ability to be able to laugh at yourself. It helps to keep your mental balance. A person with a sense of humor almost always has a good personality, and a sense of humor will help you in your association with others.

It is noteworthy that the dictator type of mind is almost invariably devoid of humor. Napoleon, for example, completely lacked a sense of humor, and so did Hitler. Dictators are often notoriously lacking in the ability to laugh at themselves, and as a result are unable to see themselves in a true perspective.

Many people are born with the potentialities of a good personality, but these are not allowed to develop normally. Can you imagine a baby entirely without them? He has the elementary mannerisms of smiling at you and reaching for your hand. If he does, you are enchanted with him, which is just another way of saying that he has personality.

The next step in personality development is that of playing with and getting along with other children. Don't overlook the fact that up to this point both parents and nurses have generally done everything to make this next step difficult by pampering and petting the child and satisfying his every whim. Therefore he is ill-equipped to cope successfully with other children and may meet experiences which will further drive his personality inward. And so it goes. As he enters school he continues to meet increasingly difficult situations. At every turn are possible frustrations. Do not forget that fear is present in practically all of our relations with others. Fear of being made a fool of, fear of losing what we have, or fear of bodily harm.

Fear is the greatest thief of personality. We know that unpleasant experiences, expecially those that happen rather early in life, tend to make people withdraw into themselves. Psychologists call such people *introverts;* the outgoing type, the one with the ability to meet other people more easily, is the *extrovert.*

Do you know which type you are? Do not get the idea that one type is necessarily superior to the other. They are different, that is all, and each is as necessary in the world as the other. Most people, moreover, combine a little of both types and even the most introverted can, with intelligent effort, develop certain of the characteristics of the extrovert. The best way to help such people is to encourage them to become skilled in activities that throw them into contact with others. If you are inclined to be shy, which after all, is nothing but fear of other people, try to become skilled in golf, tennis, bridge, backgammon, or other games. This will afford you an easy way to mingle with other people and help you to get over the feeling that others don't want you around.

One shy young man of my acquaintance obtained a job one summer selling cosmetics from house to house. He told me that the first week he could hardly muster up the courage to ring any doorbells at all, but would just walk up one street and down another. But he stuck to it, and, as the weeks passed, his shyness disappeared and the experience gave him the self-confidence his personality needed.

If you do not possess and cannot develop an outgoing personality, there are certain fields of endeavor you will be wise to avoid. It is hard to find a more unhappy person than the introvert who is trying to make good at a job which requires a good deal of intercourse with people, such as selling, advertising, politics, and practically all executive work. On the other hand, the mistake is often made of putting strongly extroverted people in jobs entirely unsuited to them.

Don't be afraid to be an introvert. Find the field that is suitable for you and don't try to do the work of an extrovert. Much of the imaginative, creative work in business is done by the introvert.

A very attractive young man, who came from a small town in Texas, wanted to make his way in New York and went there as soon as he had been graduated from college. After ten years he realized that he was doing only moderately well. In the central office of a large chain store where he was employed, he saw man after man promoted over his head. At length he had a long talk with the personnel man about why he was stagnating in spite of his hard work.

The personnel director was, fortunately, an understanding sort of man. He listened patiently, while the young man poured out his troubles. "What is the matter with me?" concluded the Texan.

There was nothing the matter with his work, the personnel director told him. He had an attractive personality and he was generally liked. The difficulty was that he was not forceful enough. He could not get his ideas across to groups of people. When managers from the chain stores met, he was not sufficiently dominating to make them understand what he thought should be done.

The young Texan thought it over and came to the conclusion that the personnel man's appraisal had been a good one. Finally he gave up his New York position and opened a store in a small town in Texas. He made a signal success of it because he knew his business. His store did not require the dominating qualities, the lack of which had prevented his success in a big organization. He learned, in other words, to use what he had, not to handicap himself any longer by letting his shortcomings stand in his way. Wisely he chose a job where they didn't matter.

Another important aspect of your personality is *tact.* This is the ability to deal adroitly and diplomatically with other people. Forceful and egotistical people are very often lacking in tact and they are apt to rub others the wrong way. People without force generally have tact because they are anxious not to offend others. Strong and aggressive people do not necessarily want to be offensive, but they may be because they are sometimes unaware of the feelings of others.

I know a bond salesman who did not achieve the success his ability deserved because of his lack of tact. His effectiveness as a salesman was amazing with people whose standards were the same as his, but when he approached his more important accounts, he never seemed to get anywhere. Finally his chief decided to make a trip with him to see what was wrong. He understood the reason immediately when he saw his boorish, back-slapping approach to important officers of banks and insurance companies. This method worked wonders with those who cared for such boisterous friendliness, but was obviously offensive to those who didn't. There are many such instances, some obvious and some subtle. Many people do not realize that their progress is greatly hampered because of their lack of adequate tact.

It may be fitting here to say a few words about *good manners,* because they are a definite skill of personality.

I am afraid that they have been rather neglected of late years. There is almost a tendency, indeed, to specialize in bad manners. But it cannot be overemphasized that good manners are very essential in modern business. A boorish attitude toward one's secretary or one's subordinates, or a grouchy or unfriendly one to other employees, is entirely out of fashion. It takes very little experience in business to teach the college graduate that while careless manners were understood by college classmates, they are not accepted with good grace by associates in business. It may be a good idea, therefore, to polish up your manners.

The qualities of personality which I have been discussing deal to some extent with the externals. There is another quality which, honestly estimated, can reveal to you whether or not you are a good buy for an employer. That is the quality of your personality which is revealed by your *standards.*

Suppose you take a look at these standards. Other people are going to judge you by them, because they are one of the most important indications of your character. Character, indeed, depends on the moral fiber you inherited and on the standards you have developed for yourself. If these standards are high and well-defined, and you have habitually used them, you are almost certain to make better progress than a person of low standards.

Too often standards seem unimportant. The easygoing quality of our present era is apt to be very misleading, and we fall into the habit of doing the things that require the least effort. But standards take effort. To create the right ones requires the most terrific struggle all your life. The effort, of course, is much too great for the majority and they give up the fight even before they start.

A person of character and ability *always* has standards: standards of conduct, of performance, and of values; standards of speech and of judgement. Some of these are acquired consciously and some unconsciously. Some he learns himself, and some were bred into him as a youngster by his parents and teachers. Some he achieves through his successes and some he learns by his failures and disappointments. The elements of effort, strife, and even suffering is always present in the process, which probably explains why the weak and spineless fall by the wayside. In any case, the worthwhile person—the person of strong character, good motivation, and proper attitudes—sets high standards for himself and strives to live up to them.

From the waitress who places the knives and forks in the wrong place to the head of a company who permits careless work on the part of his subordinates, we have examples of low standards. The main difference between the independent grocery store and the chain is not so much one of savings from mass buying, as it is that the chain-store manager is taught higher standards of cleanliness, management, and storekeeping. A supervisor arrives each week and checks him up if he falls short. The independent merchant, however, has no one checking up on him and consequently he is apt to fall into shiftless habits of storekeeping, allowing dirt to accumulate on his goods and shelves, or overlooking the fact that he is out of wanted merchandise.

I recall the warehouse of a prominent variety store in New York City where the floors were so clean that, as in the proverbial Dutch household, one could literally eat off them. A large mail-order company keeps its stocks, from dresses to horse collars, so beautifuly lined up on its shelves, on which no dust is ever allowed to accumulate, that it is a wonder to all visitors. These things are done to promote efficiency. It is less work to keep the place clean and the stock orderly, than it is to have to dust every item as it is pulled out of stock.

Primary among personal standards is *honesty*. Honesty, although some people seem to doubt it, is still the best policy. False advertising and exaggerated selling claims are great evils, but I think it can truthfully be said that business is more honest today than ever before, and that honest men, on the whole, succeed in business.

Direct lying, of course, is relatively rare. It is the half-truth or the quarter-truth that is the usual technique. It is also a common fault to either overemphasize or to leave out certain factors; when this occurs, people often salve their consciences with the excuse that they have not directly told an untruth. But if you expect others to take you at your word and trust your statements, it is wise to present the real, honest, and unemphasized facts.

Intellectual honesty is thinking honestly. Many people who are money-honest are either misled by their own prejudices or feel that the end justifies the means, and are not above twisting meanings or confusing issues so that they may gain their ends. There are many examples of this in political life, where the necessity of being elected will make people who are normally honest, become intellectually dishonest. Men in business, too, are sometimes blinded by their eagerness to conclude some business transaction and overlook those principles of honesty which they would never permit their own sons to ignore.

These things are not always done deliberately, but our psychological make-up is such that we are prone to grasp at those straws which are favorable to our own interests and to minimize those that are not. Many people are so full of prejudices that it is impossible for them to be honest with themselves. Others have such zeal for some cause or purpose that they blind themselves to an honest conception of the whole. Honesty with one's self is a rare quality. Strictly speaking, no one is entirely honest with himself, because he is afraid to see himself as he really is. Nevertheless, honesty with yourself is a very important attribute if you hope to be charged with responsibility over other people.

Find Out What You've Got

How able a person are you? What kind of ability have you? What are your aptitudes? These are questions which other people, particularly those who will eventually use your services, will constantly try to determine. The conclusions they reach will by no means be absolutely accurate, *but they will act on them just the same.* You will go through your business life surrounded by this sea of other people's opinions, but you will often be the last to be aware of what they are. These other people will not tell you, as a rule. Some because they don't want to hurt your feelings, and some because they don't want to be bothered, but generally because you don't want to hear about them anyway.

You alone, all too often, have not tried to make a realistic and constructive appraisal of yourself. As, after all, you must market what you have, isn't it foolish to allow your prospective buyers to have a more accurate evaluation of you than you have of yourself?

Since your progress in business will depend to a considerable extent on the accuracy of your analysis of yourself, it is necessary for you to tackle such an evaluation as carefully as possible. It isn't an easy job. The first stumbling block is that you are human and like to look at yourself in a favorable light. Our mental picture of what we are generally leaves out most of our faults and builds our virtues to great heights.

If you are to arrive at anything like an accurate estimate of your own abilities and aptitudes, which will help you in planning intelligently for your future, you must be as brutally honest with yourself as it is possible to be. Your conclusions should be supplemented with help from others who are not as emotionally involved as you are. Remember that our knowledge of psychology and human behaviour is extremely limited. And it is not possible to make a definite quantitative or qualitative analysis as is done in chemistry. Nevertheless, you must make some sort of evaluation, and not be afraid to change it as you learn more about yourself.

Now it is extremely difficult, of course, for any person to estimate his own *intelligence.* As a matter of fact, it is often true that the more intelligent a person is the less intelligent he thinks he is, and the stupider he is, the more intelligent he believes himself to be.

It is, of course, obvious that the quality of your intelligence has a great bearing on your progress in business. Naturally, the intelligent person will do better than the stupid one. There are, however, many other factors that must be taken into consideration. Basic intelligence is only one of them and that, as I have pointed out, is a quality which is difficult for you to estimate for yourself.

The one factor which is of even more importance to you is the *direction of your intelligence,* and this is a determinable quality.

Some people are intelligent in one direction, some in

another. A mathematics scholar may be a wizard in algebra or calculus, for example, but his intelligence on artistic matters may be practically zero. If you are a good sprinter and can run 100 yards in 10 flat, but you are light and haven't much ability for shifting your weight, you don't try to be a football player, do you? The same thing applies in the mental field.

Very few people are intelligent in more than one or two directions. Almost none have what might be termed multi-directional intelligence. You probably know people who are highly intelligent at bridge, for example, and yet who seem to be positively stupid about other things, and the reverse, of course, is also true.

A friend of mine made a brilliant record as a colonel in the Army. He was generally conceded to be one of the ablest commanding officers in Europe. But when he tried to fit himself into a business career after the war, he was unable to make a success of anything. His intelligence was high when directed toward military matters, but low when directed toward business matters. On the other hand, there have been many military leaders who have also been highly intelligent in business.

But here is a reassuring and highly encouraging fact. Nearly everyone is intelligent along some particular line. The recognition of this basic principle is of the utmost importance in the choice of your vocation, because it will play a major role in your future progress. Its proper application makes it possible for many more people to do well in business than would be the case if general intelligence were the only determining factor. In fact, I have seen many men do extremely well because they chose an occupation which was eminently suited to their intelligence. As a matter of fact, some of them were stupid in other directions, but their usefulness was not impaired by this because the occupation they chose required the type of intelligence they possessed.

Very often people who have a high degree of intelligence along mechanical lines find it almost impossible to understand anything about human relations. I know a brilliant engineer who became the head of a large company, and because of his lack of intelligence in his relationships with those below him, caused his company to be constantly distressed by strikes and other personnel difficulties. Another man rose to great heights in the oil business because of his unusual ability in the refining field, but he was completely unintelligent about financial matters. His refinery was the envy of everyone in the industry, and people came to admire its efficiency, but when it came to finance, his ideas were fantastic and impractical, and it wasn't long before these ideas ruined him. If he had listened to his advisors, who had more understanding of finance than he, he would still be in business today.

In other words, if you are typical, you will find that you are smarter in some directions than in others. This does not mean that you shouldn't continue to broaden your horizon in every possible way, but it does mean that if you can place yourself in an endeavor to which your particular type of intelligence is most suited, you will have an obvious advantage over other people whose intelligence may not be as suitable for it as yours.

Specialization is so great in business today that there is a constant effort being made to try and fit people into the proper niches. Why isn't the individual trying—why aren't you trying—to make a similar effort to fit yourself into your right place? Certainly, it is as important to you as it is to business that you find the place where you can do the best work. Consciously or unconsciously, there is a continual reshuffling going on, shifting men and women from place to place in an attempt to find the right one, and yet those who are being moved about in this fashion appear to be almost unaware of the process. They seem to wait, in a sort of fog, for someone else to find the right place for them.

I am constantly staggered by this passive waiting for someone else to do for you what you should be doing for yourself. "Why should I figure out what I am good for, what I can do best?" you seem to ask. "That's the personnel man's job. He'll decide where I fit in. After all, am I supposed to know the doctor's reasons when he decides I have appendicitis? It's his job, isn't it?"

This mental inertia is accountable for a great deal of wasted effort and lost opportunity today in business. The high degree of specialization which has developed in the business structure offers more opportunity than ever to the person of average ability. And this is an important point which is too often overlooked.

The modern world is built to the scale of the average man. It's his oyster. But, it's up to him to open it.

The hit-or-miss process can't be recommended as a method of getting anywhere, of achieving anything. If you don't want to get lost in a big corporation, give yourself an intelligent chance by figuring out for yourself where you can fit in and aim for it.

Well, then, how are you going to find out what you can do best? One young man told me what he had done. He said that his father, who was a professional man without business experience, was unable to advise him as to how to find his proper niche. Being an understanding man, however, he suggested that the boy make a list of a dozen men in different types of businesses.

"Don't go to these men in search of a job," he said,

"but ask them instead to give you some advice. Most older men feel complimented when they are asked for advice by younger men or women. Tell them about yourself and ask them whether they can see anything in you that might make you useful in their business."

It took the boy about two months to see all twelve men, but it was worth it. As soon as they understood that it was not necessary to turn him away with excuses, they talked at length. They advised him about the pitfalls in their businesses. They sketched for him, roughly, the types of men who seemed to do well, those who failed, and what it took to get ahead.

This story interested me so much that I discussed it with the president of a prominent university. I suggested to him a similar plan, done on a larger scale. The plan was to select a panel of several hundred graduates, to be divided into committees of five people each. They were to promise to devote one week each year to the work. The names of these people would be posted in the dean's office with the time they had promised to serve. Undergraduates who wished to avail themselves of the privilege could come to talk to all five of them by making arrangements through the dean's office. The students were not to come seeking jobs, but to find out what was needed in that person's business. I am convinced that some such system would be of great benefit to college undergraduates, and I believe likewise that the time so spent would be of benefit to the people on the committee.

So get in touch with people in various types of businesses in your own community, explain your problem to them, and ask their advice. What do their businesses need? Into what types of activities are they divided? What qualities do these people need in the men and women they employ? What type of people do they prefer?

Their answers to these questions will give you rating cards of your own by which to measure what you have and what is required.

Another method is to make experiments by working during summer vacations. This should be done objectively, with thoughtful analysis. Try to determine, for example, the kind of work you think you are fitted and then get such a job during the summer. If this is done during the freshman year, there will be ample time to analyze the results during the sophomore year. Then try some other kind of work the next summer.

This affords an opportunity to experiment with three or four classifications of work activities in different industries, and will give you an immense advantage over those who have not made such experiments.

I recall one person who did this and who told me that he had been discharged from an accounting firm where he had worked during the summer. He insisted on being told why he was discharged, and was informed that he was too slow with figures, very inaccurate in his addition, and altogether unsuited to be an accountant. This galled him at first, but gradually he began to understand that he was not suited for the work, and decided that after graduation he would give it a wide berth.

Whatever else you gain from these summer jobs, by these experiments you will at least learn the answers to some of the questions I asked Garver when he came to me—the questions that someone will ask you.

Do You Know Your Inner Self?

What do you know about your *emotional makeup?* Your feelings play as important a part as your mind in your business career, and therefore it is essential that they be normal, healthy, and well balanced. If they are not, you are apt to be prejudiced, badly balanced, or emotionally unstable. Such a person is not a good risk in business, and although he may have a fair share of brains and ability, his emotional instability makes it dangerous to place responsibility in his hands. I have seen too many examples of this.

I recall an instance where an emotionally unstable man was placed in charge of a shoe factory. Almost immediately the home office began to have trouble with the plant. Labor difficulties, resignations of executives, and quarrels of all kinds seemed to be the rule. Investigation disclosed that an otherwise efficient factory had been completely demoralized because of the manager's emotional outbursts. He was unfair with his people, often without meaning to be. He was quick to anger and vented his wrath upon his subordinates. His emotional instability, of course, affected his judgement, as it always does.

It is difficult for emotionally unstable people to see things as they really are. They seem to take everything personally, which makes it extremely difficult to use them effectively in business. Part of this lack of *emotional integration,* however, is caused by poor training by parents and teachers during the formative years. If parental discipline is lacking and the child is spoiled, it becomes difficult, if not impossible, to achieve integration later on in life. Too many people make the mistake of thinking that discipline is only of chief importance in regulating a child's external life and fail to see that by far its more important function is to help him arrive at proper emotional integration.

It is, therefore, necessary to appraise your degree of integration and emotional stability in order to determine not only the kind of work which will be suitable for you, but also the amount of responsibility you will be able to assume.

Even normally well-integrated people find it necessary to exercise emotional control. This does not necessarily indicate instability. It has rather to do with *emotional maturity.* An emotionally mature person learns to control emotions.

Highly emotional people are often very valuable in certain kinds of activities. They are apt to be creative and imaginative. Don't think that emotional people have no place in business. But it is a fact that those who aspire to responsible executive jobs must have emotional maturity.

More people than we generally suspect have infantile emotional reactions. Almost everyone has them at times. But the emotionally mature person has them rather seldom. I have heard it said by competent authorities that almost thirty percent of the people in business today are immature emotionally. One of the most frequent manifestations of this in business is the habit of letting your judgement of others be influenced by your likes or dislikes. This is a common practice and a very dangerous one. After all, a person's efficiency, intelligence, and ability can hardly be measured accurately by such a method. Yet there are many men, some in responsible positions too, who have built their whole organizations in this way.

Healthy emotions, on the other hand, are a great help to intelligence. As a matter of fact, *intuition,* which is a very valuable quality, probably rests largely on emotions. There are some people who seem to be endowed with intuition to more than an ordinary degree. A friend of mine who is unusually intuitive told me the following story:

"I sat next to the famous Ivar Kreuger, the Swedish Match King, on his first visit to the United States, and almost before I engaged him in conversation, a shock of great aversion passed through me. As the luncheon progressed it grew stronger, and I could hardly wait until the meal was over. Later when people tried to interest me in some of his companies, I refused to have anything to do with them because my aversion to the man himself made me reluctant to be connected with him in any way. As a result, I also advised several influential people not to make any investments in Mr. Kreuger's many enterprises. Later developments, of course, proved that my feelings had been correct."

Some able businessmen have combined intuition with rational reasoning to an extraordinary extent. An example of this occurred during the bank moratorium of 1933. It was at a meeting of executives of one of the country's great mail-order companies. The meeting had been called to discuss the problem of what to do with the millions of dollars' worth of orders containing bank checks that were no longer negotiable due to the closing of the banks.

It was pointed out by the treasurer of the company and concurred in by almost everyone present that it would be ruinous to fill all these orders because the checks were no longer good. It was variously suggested that the orders be held up and the checks returned to their owners.

One of the executives present at the meeting insisted, however, that the orders must be filled immediately and the worthless checks returned with a note of explanation in each package. The note would explain, he said, why the checks were being included and would request that the recipients return either cash or money orders.

The other executives objected strenuously and pointed out that the company might conceivably lose millions of dollars.

"Even if it does," he maintained, "although my intuition tells me that it will not, the good will of the company is at stake. We must not allow all these people who have trusted us for years to think that at this crucial time we refuse to trust them."

It is interesting to note that though the discussion continued for three days, he finally won his point. The goods were all shipped and the checks returned with a note, explaining the situation.

The response was slow as might have been expected with the country practically without cash and small banks going into bankruptcy by the thousands. But finally the answers began to pour in and this man's intuition and faith in the general honesty of the American people was eventually justified. Out of all these millions of dollars' worth of orders, the final loss amounted only to the ridiculous figure of a little over $15,000.

There is another factor which is very important and that is *maturity of mind.* How old are you mentally? It must be realized that you have a mental age as well as a physical one. It is difficult for most people to realize that a person of forty may have a mental age of twenty. We are prone to be fooled by physical appearance. Just because a man is grown, we take for granted that his mind is also mature. Actually very little correlation exists between the two. Most people have a variation between their mental and physical ages. Mental maturity is often directional, that is, some people may be mentally mature in certain directions while they are immature in others. The detection of mental maturity is rather difficult, particularly for those who have had very little experience with it. It plays a very important role, however, not only in the type of work a person can do, but also in how well he can do it.

The best way to develop maturity is through responsibility. A hundred years ago when life was more primitive, and responsibility had to be shared by all members of the family, many people arrived at mental maturity at an early age. It has also been noted that people from small towns seem on the whole to be more mature mentally than those from large metropolitan centers. This is probably true because people in smaller communities are given more responsibility.

It is often the case that young men and women who come from sheltered homes lack mental maturity. It is a good practice to throw young people on their own resources as soon as possible and require them to make their own judgements and accept a certain amount of responsibility. All of this can be done with enough control and discipline so that proper guidance is always present.

How *responsible* are you? It will be worth while for you to test your own sense of responsibility; find out to what extent you make your own judgements instead of relying on others to make them for you; check back on your own activities to discover whether you have felt responsible for tasks which were left in your care. A great many people are afraid of responsibility and dodge it whenever they can. For one thing, it takes more energy to make a decision than to depend on someone else to do it for you. It has been my experience that assistants to responsible people often have the idea that the higher job is easier than the one they are doing. They are sure they could handle it with no more difficulty than the one they have. But when the promotion comes, they recoil before the responsibility which faces them. It is no longer someone else who must accept the load, take the criticism, think through the problem, and be responsible for the solution. And often they wilt when they come up against it.

Responsible jobs cannot be filled by superficial people, but demand men or women who can penetrate to the core of any problem or situation. Can you think fundamentally? A test question I have asked many times in order to illustrate this is: "What is the most basic rule in football?" I have asked it of coaches, players, and of people who have been close followers of the sport. It is a very short rule, but I have yet to meet anyone who can give it. It is so fundamental that it is always overlooked. Here is the answer. "A loose ball may not be kicked." You see, without that rule football would be totally changed. It would no longer be football as we know it, but some other game.

You may be able to think in terms of fundamentals and still lack a quality which is necessary in business—and that is *shrewdness*. I don't mean by this the most popularly recognized type of shrewdness, bargaining ability or the capacity for bargaining another down in price. Basic shrewdness goes further than that. If you have a penetrating mind, a discerning mind, a mind that is not naive and that cannot easily be swayed, you are shrewd. Shrewdness can, of course, also be of a low order, such as cunning, which is merely a malicious tendency to take advantage of others. But basic shrewdness is essential in directing others. A very important part of executive work is the ability to judge others. The very meaning of the word "executive" implies having other people work for you. It follows, therefore, that if you are going to build up a good organization, you must be able to judge others and the work they do. Many executives fail because they lack shrewdness to judge accurately either the situations that confront them or the people they are dealing with.

Another important business asset is *imagination*. It is one of the great gifts of the human race, and the basis of all creative work. But the important thing again is that imagination, like intelligence, has a directional trend. It is, therefore, extremely important for you to try to determine first, whether you have imagination, and second, what direction this ability takes. For if you lack imagination, you should avoid work that requires it.

Take for example, the work of sales management. This requires imagination to a high degree. For the sales manager creates selling ideas for his sales force, and also develops the plans to carry them out. The only management job I can think of which might not require some degree of imagination is one in which all the steps have been plotted out by some higher official, as might possibly be the case with a foreman in a warehouse or factory. Generally speaking, however, management jobs require imagination. But again, almost every type of management requires a different type of imagination.

A young friend of mine who was starting out in business used to come to me to talk over his troubles. And I say troubles advisedly, because he was getting along very badly. He was employed as a reporter on a New York newspaper and didn't like it a bit. Whenever I saw him he was tired and listless and looked as if he didn't have the strength even to talk about it. It was plain that he had no interest in his work and was only doing it because his father had been a great journalist before him and his mother was anxious to see him eventually tread in his father's footsteps.

Finally, I interceded with his mother and explained to her that her son apparently did not have the aptitude for the newspaper field, and that she should stop urging him to emulate his father and let him try to find something he was better fitted for.

With the aid of a competent psychologist, we determined after several weeks of testing and experimenting that the boy had an aptitude for two things, engineering and selling. Further conversations developed that the engineering aptitude was not strong enough to warrant his becoming an engineer. Our final conclusion was that he should go into the selling phase of something that had a strong engineering flavor.

He resigned his job with the newspaper and for several months I heard nothing from him. Then one morning he burst into my office and said he had landed a job on the West coast with a big machinery manufacturing company. He was to go to their school to learn how to sell machines.

He was a changed boy. His eyes shone and his enthusiasm bubbled over. I couldn't help contrasting his new attitude with the disinterested one he had while he was struggling to become a reporter.

This is an example of the importance of discovering your own aptitudes so that you may utilize your energy to its fullest extent. Merely expending energy, however, is a waste. There are probably hundreds of "energy scatterers" to every one with organized energy. Proper attention to, and training of, energy by utilizing concentration in the right way is most important if you wish to make effective use of your energy.

The more important the job in the business world, the more of a *mental horizon* is necessary. Do you have vision and scope and the ability to see the forest instead of the trees? Because of the rarity of this ability, it is always difficult to fill the big jobs satisfactorily.

The other day the head of a large company called me on the telephone and told me that he was dissatisfied with one of his important executives. But, he said, "We have been unable to find anyone else who would be better." He asked me as a favor to mull it over and see if I could think of men around the country who would be big enough for the job. "It would pay," he said, "one hundred thousand dollars a year and a percentage of future profits."

Although I know of several such important openings, it is an interesting fact that I know of only a few available positions which would pay two hundred dollars per week. The reason for this is that there are plenty of people with the capacity to do these smaller jobs, but the men with the mental horizon and ability necessary to do the more important ones are extremely rare. This should be encouraging to many young men who feel that opportunities in this country no longer exist. You can take my word for it that there are more opportunities, really big opportunities, than there are men to take advantage of them. There are scores of big positions today that are not filled to the satisfaction of directors of many companies. But many of these incumbents keep their jobs because it is almost impossible to find men with greater mental horizons.

One of the most vital of all qualities is that of *leadership.* As a rule, it must be developed early in life. And, in addition, skill in it must constantly be cultivated. It is surprising how few people, young or old, can give orders properly. It is a good plan to practice in your undergraduate life. If you hope to be a leader, practice saying what you have to say briefly and concisely. Organize your material so that you won't ramble on in a confusing way which only lowers the interest of your audience.

There are many ways of practicing leadership. No opportunities to do so should be overlooked. The work of counselor in camps during the summer is the type of work that will bring out leadership qualities. Campus activities that require organizing, planning, and execution should not be neglected. If your final conclusion is that you are not a leader, the wisest thing you can do is to plan the course of your life so that you can enter a field where this ability is not required. If, on the other hand, you have the ability but are too lazy to school yourself in it, you have no right to expect to be placed where it is required.

It's The Little Things That Count

Apart from the matter of individual talents, abilities, and specialized skills, there are other skills which are necessary no matter what position you take, and it would pay you to check yourself on them. These are the ordinary, simple skills: skill in arithmetic, in reading, and in writing. These may seem elementary, but because they are constantly needed in carrying out the details of any ordinary working day, it is appalling how many people handle them badly.

Little things. A disproportionate number of college men and women major in economics and are well-posted on current theories, but most of them find it difficult to add up a simple column of figures, let alone handle fractions. It is a peculiar quirk of our educational system that fractions and the old familiar problems about covering rooms with carpets that are studied in grammar school are forgotten later on when people go into business and need skills in simple arithmetic. Sometimes I feel that arithmetic should be taught again in the senior year of high school, because most people seem to have forgotten all about it by the time they graduate. The modern eagerness to depend on pocket computers may be more of a handicap than some young people think.

Speaking clearly, coherently, and properly is also a skill not possessed by many people. And yet it is basic and absolutely essential if you desire to make progress in business. There are extraordinarily few men and women in business today who can speak clearly and forcefully. I am not referring just to public speaking. Obviously that is a valuable skill if you can acquire it, and it is usually possible to get considerable experience and practice in public speaking in college. The essential thing, however, is the ability to express your ideas clearly, coherently, and with confidence when talking to small groups of people.

Most of the planning, presenting, and deciding on ideas is done verbally in meetings of small groups of men and women. The person who can present ideas the most effectively has an immeasurable advantage over the person who wanders from the point, who hesitates and fumbles and appears to lack faith in his or her own ideas.

Here I would like to say a word about proper *enunciation*. Careless, sloppy English detracts from the effectiveness of what you say, and lowers the estimate others have of you and of your potentialities. Slovenly speech brands you as a person more anxious to appear indistinguishably one of the crowd than to be of some significance. It stamps you as lacking in a desire to grow.

It is this tendency which is strikingly revealed in the contrast between those who follow the ideals of the Boy Scouts, where the whole process is one of rising step by step, learning to excel in various fields, and those who follow the gang where the process is one of leveling everyone to a common, and very low, standard. Careless

43

speech will always reveal you to the observant employer as belonging to this latter type, and the wise employer is careful never to place too much leadership responsibility in the hands of a person who displays this trait.

Skill in *reading* implies not only speed, but also the ability to read aloud with the proper emphasis, with clarity, with forcefulness; these abilities are most important when reading a paper to an audience. It is important to devote some time to practicing these skills when you have the opportunity, because there is nothing more pitiful than to see a man stammer and stumble when reading a paper, mumbling the words, throwing the accent in the wrong places, losing the interest of the people, and nullifying the effect of what he says, however carefully it may have been prepared.

In business it is more important to be able to speak well than it is to be able to write well, though it is also necessary to be able to write clearly and forcefully. This does not mean that it is necessary to cultivate a literary style, although for certain businesses—advertising, publishing, and so on—such ability is extremely necessary and there is always room for people who possess it.

It amazes me how standards of proper dressing have degenerated in recent years. Such things as dirty shoes and spot-stained trousers are commonly worn by undergraduates. They seem to take pride in being dressed in as slovenly a fashion as possible. These habits will not help them establish the standards they must develop in order to become presentable people in business.

Appearance is important, as you can learn from anyone who has tried to find a job. Aside from the superficial aspects of appearance, such as clothes, and so forth, your appearance must reflect calmness, alertness, poise, and self confidence, so that you may gain the respect of your co-workers as well as your superiors. It is obvious that these things are necessary if you aspire to a position of leadership.

Failure to pay attention to what is being said to you is a common shortcoming. Perhaps you are in a hurry, or you are thinking about something which seems more important, or you are merely absent-minded. The fact remains that you haven't listened, and this is immediately apparent to the acute observer. Aside from the fact that you may have misunderstood the instructions by inattentiveness, or that you may blunder as a result of it, no one likes to feel that what he says arouses neither interest nor response.

If you will turn back to the list of questions for rating salespeople, you will see that a number of them are concerned with the ordinary skills, with the little things, which, added up, determine a person's standards of performance. Speed. Accuracy. Orderliness. They are not brilliant qualities, but they are fundamentally important in the day-by-day duties of a job. And they are too often overlooked.

By cultivating these fundamental skills you will gradually make yourself a more disciplined and a more efficient employee, and the efficient employee is the valuable employee. Such people do not often have to look for jobs; the jobs are looking for them.

Continuing Education

Do not make the mistake of thinking that the purpose of education is merelyto prepare you to earn your living. Education is designed, rather, to broaden you as a person. I know a man who studied philosophy and English literature while he was in college to prepare himself for a business career. This was so vastly different from the usual procedure of studying economics that he was asked what his reasons had been in choosing courses that were commonly considered intellectual rather than practical. His answer was that he had decided to use his college education to prepare himself for the higher rungs of the business ladder.

"If I prepare myself for the lower rungs alone," he said, "how will I be ready to meet my problems if I should be fortunate enough to reach the higher ones? After all, it seems to me that the more responsible duties will be infinitely more difficult to discharge and it is, therefore, important for me to make greater preparation for them. I will take my chance that I will get through the smaller responsibilities somehow. If I don't, it doesn't make any difference anyway."

This viewpoint of education seems to be rather overlooked by many men and women graduating today, who do not know that the country is in much greater need of leaders with the foresight to prepare themselves adequately for larger responsibilities.

The wrong kind of preparation for a business career is being made today by a vast majority of undergraduates. They seem to feel that majoring in economics is the best way to fit themselves for commercial life. Consequently, we have seen an ever-growing number of students forsaking the arts and sciences, not to mention literature and history, to take more and more courses in economics.

A prominent university discovered that among its nine hundred students in the senior class, only three had majored in philosophy, only seven in mathematics and none in the classics. An overwhelming percentage had majored in economics, showing the extent to which the specialized education idea had been carried.

But, you say, it seems reasonable to specialize in economics if you're going into business. It sounds plausible, but actually it isn't. For example, in the same university, it was found that of the two graduates who had achieved the greatest success in the legal field, neither had taken any pre-law work as undergraduates; the three most prominent doctors had taken no pre-medical courses while in college; the most prominent banker had majored in English and had taken only three hours of economics. Of two well-known merchants who were alumni of the university, neither of them had majored in economics, but one had devoted himself to philosophy and the other to history, with only two and one-third courses in economics. In other words, all of these men had used their college educations to help them develop a broad cultural background, rather than merely to train themselves in certain narrow fields. This served them in good stead when they were called upon to meet their heavy responsibilities later on in life.

One function of your college education, as I see it, is not so much to fit you for a job, as to help you discover what kind of career you are fitted for. After you have learned this, you can start training for it at any time. Naturally, the sooner you can discover your particular bent, the sooner you can start focusing your energies and acquiring the specialized knowledge which that particular field requires. A friend of mine, one of the best-known publishers in the country, told me that he knew he wanted to be a newspaper man when he was ten years old. And, although he obtained a general education as well as a law degree, he molded it all to fit his purpose.

I have noticed time and again that once the diploma is acquired, there is a tendency to consider that the problem of education has been solved, and that nothing more need be done about it. This attitude leads straight to mental stagnation. It is the people with the constant urge for self-improvement who forge ahead. I recall the case of a young man who was anxious to get a certain promotion. The position required a person of some education and it developed that he had only two years of high school. This was brought to his attention and he learned his lesson so well that he made great efforts thereafter to increase his education and improve himself.

A great violinist was once asked how many lessons he had taken before he could play so beautifully. " 'Taken'?" he answered. "I am still taking them."

The continuing education is essential to growth. The

mind, like the muscles, has to be kept pliable by constant use. Some of the Indian fakirs hold one arm in the air, without using it, until it shrivels up. The mind which is unused becomes valueless. Behind you there is a constantly renewed group of younger, alert, eager minds ready to take your place. And if you remember the Red Queen's advice, you must run as fast as you can even to stay in the same place.

The means are at hand for the person who wishes to continue his education, more so today than at any time in the past. The public libraries, the radio, television, the university extension courses, offer immediate and inexpensive ways of opening up new fields of information, or of perfecting yourself in those you have already discovered. Opportunities abound to enable you to become an expert craftsman in your field.

So far as perfecting yourself in your own craft or trade is concerned, there is a growing realization on the part of business and the labor unions that such a process is of overwhelming importance. Business through the training of its personnel, unions through special classes for their members, are both trying to develop in employees the essential skills of their trades, skills which too many people are now lacking.

It must be realized that one's education is never over, that school and college are merely groundwork, and that after graduation you really begin your education. This attitude is not generally understood. Too many feel that when college is over there will be no more homework and the days will be spent in pleasant duties and the evenings in endless enjoyment. This attitude is deplorable and, no doubt, contributes to the general lowering of the moral fiber of this country.

Before a college education became such a general

thing, people seemed to be more imbued with this urge of self-improvement. It furnishes the people who have it with a strong drive. It manifests itself in many ways. The desire to be better educated and to improve your position in life are only a few of the many forms it takes. It is always present as a great driving force among worthwhile people, and if you are lacking in it, you can take it for granted that you will not go far.

In my own case, I found that although I had taken several courses in college on the appreciation of art and painting, I was still so lacking in real knowledge of it, that I spent four years going to the Metropolitan Museum of Art in New York City, where New York University's courses in art history were then given. The courses were about period furniture, antique silver, and rugs, color, design, painting, textile design, and so forth.

Unfortunately, however, during the process of equipping yourself for a life in business, nine out of ten of you are apt to overlook the element which is becoming daily of increasing importance, the matter of developing design judgment.

Of late years there has been a growing necessity for everyone to develop standards in esthetics. This has to do with design, line, proportion, color, scale, and mass. This is not the time to go deeply into esthetics, but we must scan it enough to indicate its importance.

It is generally studied only superficially in college. But an understanding of it is becoming essential in so many lines of business that there are few positions where some knowledge of it is not of great value.

You probably feel that you have inherent taste and that studying the subject is a waste of time. This may be so in a few instances, but in the vast majority of cases, taste is an acquired set of standards. I have met many people who feel insulted if it is suggested that their taste is poor.

My advice is that universities all over the country should give this subject a great deal more thought. It is also my feeling that many undergraduate courses are too academic, too theoretical, and that it is almost impossible for students to take a proper group of courses which would lay the groundwork for their appreciation of esthetics. Those who are lacking in design judgement, or who have not bothered to acquire it, should studiously avoid certain businesses.

The truth is that the consuming public, not only in large metropolitan centers, but also in small towns and on farms, is increasingly demanding that everything they buy be better looking. My experience in selling to such people has convinced me of this. The reason is that the American woman has educated herself in matters of taste in the past twenty years. If companies supplying her wants do not give her what she demands she will go elsewhere. If the men running these companies do not wake up, they will find themselves far behind the procession.

Getting Down to Brass Tacks

Once a young man came in to see me and said he had been looking around for a job for three or four months. I asked him what he had been doing and it developed that he was looking for a job when he had nothing else to do, when it didn't interfere with his social engagements, and when he didn't sleep too late after a party.

"I'll give you a job right now," I told him, "a nine to five job like any other. Your job is getting a job. Get up in the morning and start your rounds at nine o'clock. Don't knock off half the day for lunch, or take off the afternoon to enjoy yourself. Stick at it, every day, all day, working as hard and as consistently at it as you would at any other assignment."

He walked out of my office rather disgusted, but five days later he called me up, and in a voice which indicated he hardly believed it himself, told me that the method had worked and he had found a job.

I am not trying to dodge the fact that this is one of the hardest problems that faces you. However, it is something you must do for yourself. There's no overlooking the present unemployment problem, there's no ignoring the competition you meet in every field. But if you have intelligently prepared to face these conditions, if you start out with no foolish illusions as to what you will find, if you will map out some sort of goal for yourself and direct your forces and abilities wisely, you'll have a better chance than the next applicant for the job.

A good general makes a plan of campaign before he goes into battle. He would not, for example, attempt to attack an enemy without thinking out all the possibilities very carefully in advance, so that he would have a reasonable and intelligent chance of approaching his objective successfully.

The first battle you have to win is that of getting a job. You have to figure out in advance how to storm that citadel. Why, then, approach it without having plans?

A few years ago a graduate of a School of Business Administration came to see me. He wanted to work for Montgomery Ward, of which I was at that time an officer. He whipped out a notebook and said: "These are the reasons why I believe I should do well in your company," and he gave me, clearly and forcefully and tersely, a quick resumé of the experience he had had.

Then he said: "I have been studying your company for the past year and these are the things that seem to me necessary if this company is to be reorganized successfully." It happened that at the time Montgomery Ward was going through a complete reorganization. He had informed himself of this fact. His arguments were so intelligent, he knew the problems so clearly, that there was nothing for me to do but find a job for him. As a matter of fact, he had a better understanding of the situation than employees who had been with the company for many years but had not looked beyond the problems of their immediate jobs.

Unhappily, this is one of the few examples of men who have come to me with their campaigns carefully worked out in advance. I cannot say too strongly: *Make a plan of attack!* You've selected the field for which you are fitted. You are familiar with the reasons which fit you for it. Practice them. Rehearse them. *Learn to sell yourself!* Then when you talk to the personnel director or to the employment manager, you will be able to discuss them swiftly, coherently, and with conviction.

Of course, if you are the kind of person who drags himself from one employment office to another, that's another matter. But if you know your business—and your business is getting yourself the right job—you must know your reasons for your choice. If you can't put them forward with conviction, practice them until you can.

If, after you have been your most persuasive, the personnel director turns you down, try to find out his reasons. Ask him frankly whether he thinks you are on the wrong track, whether, in his opinion, you should not try to enter his kind of business. If you can persuade him to do this, the refusal will, at least, carry with it some concrete information about yourself, even if it is only one man's opinion. After the interview, write down his comments and study them. Suppose you go to ten employment directors and five of them have given their reasons for refusing you. You will have a very valuable index of your personal shortcomings from their point of view, a valuable guide in analyzing yourself and preparing yourself for a job.

On the other hand, the personnel manager may say that you are all right but that there just aren't any jobs. In that case, keep after him, don't expect him to follow you up. Don't be afraid to follow him up. On your next visit (or in your letter, if you prefer to write, though you are more apt to be remembered if you make a personal appearance) use a little strategy. Before following him up learn more about him, about his company, about the kind of business he is in. There's no point in following up with a "Well, here I am again" attitude. Have some definite point in mind, something you have learned about yourself every time you see him. But, above all, don't say, as I have so often heard, "Honestly, if you give me a chance, I will make good for you". You mean well, you are willing, anxious to make good, but such a remark is stupid because you are not in a position to guarantee such a matter.

Keep on plugging. The first thing a backfield man learns is this: No matter what happens, keep on moving your legs. It doesn't matter whether you are tackled. It doesn't matter whether you are knocked down. Keep moving!

But don't move aimlessly. Do it with a plan. If you can't do that, how can you expect to make good when you get a job? Because you'll need a plan for that, too.

Suppose the thing you have selected as the right field for you is the publishing business. You've made the rounds and there are no jobs available in the publishing field. What then? Give it up and decide to get what you can in any line? That's giving up the battle before the first clash of arms.

Whatever the industry or the trade or the craft which you have selected, there are apt to be allied businesses which are similar in their purposes and functions. The man who wants to go into a publishing house has not exhausted the possibilities until he has tried these allied fields; in this case, magazines, trade journals, newspapers, printing plants, book stores, to list only a few examples. In any one of these and in all of them he can learn invaluable information and get training which will be useful to him in a publishing house. It is all part of his apprenticeship, and part of his well-thought-out plan. When the opening does occur in the publishing house he will have something concrete to sell, practical experience in some aspect of publishing.

One man with a great deal of ingenuity found an effective way to prepare himself for this business of facing a prospective employer. Realizing that he had failed in some way to meet the requirements of various personnel men who had interviewed him, he decided to practice on his friends. Instead of rehearsing with them as a prospective employee, however, he staged interviews in which he took the part of the employer and asked his friends the questions which had been put to him.

By studying their replies and their attitudes, he was able to grasp something of the interviewer's point of view. As a result, when he faced his next interview he was quick on the trigger and made a better impression than he had before, because he had a better insight into what the employer was seeking. By this system, also, he was able to overcome a great deal of the nervousness which frequently puts the job seeker at a disadvantage and makes him give a poorer impression than he would otherwise.

Another aid in preparing for the employment interview would be to refer back to the rating questions for salesclerks and copywriters. Make a similar list of questions for the type of job you want. Spend some time at it, not five minutes, but weeks, if necessary. Do a little research, so that you can construct for yourself a reasonably complete questionnaire on the requirements of the job you want. With these in hand, you can check yourself against them, and you can also provide yourself with some powerful arguments as to why you will make a good salesclerk, copywriter, plumber, banker, librarian, or anything else you may want to be.

Let us suppose now that you have climbed your first hurdle and have found your job—not just any job, but *your* job. What are you going to do with it? The personnel man has added you to the payroll. You've been assigned to a task. It is apt to be a routine sort of job in the beginning, probably pretty dull in spots, and it lasts, as a rule, from nine to five. Those aren't school hours; the routine isn't apt to have breaks like those for changes of classes; there isn't a field where you can knock off for sports; and there won't be much glamour to it.

It isn't what you expected, is it? You are more tired than you expectedto be at the end of the day, being a subordinate taking orders seems like being a private in the army, and you discover that there are a lot of people between you and the jobs higher up, the ones which seem more stimulating, more interesting, the ones which will give you a chance to show what you can do. And just by looking around you, you can find a number of things that you think are being done wrong, things you could set right.

Unlike the acquaintances of your school days, the people among whom you are to work from now on are not likely to share your interests; they may not strike you as being particularly congenial. Find out something about them. What are they like under the surface? Learning to get along with them pleasantly is part of your job, and if you make a reasonable effort it should not be difficult. Petty jealousies and nagging disputes over details are a stupid waste of time and they can almost always be avoided, if you want to avoid them. If you have a chip on your shoulder, you'd better knock it off before you go to work.

Getting off to a bad start isn't necessarily fatal, if you can learn by your mistakes. But there are a number of young people who never learn to make that difficult adjustment to the business world as it exists, the ones who know they could get along all right if things were different, if they had other people to work with, other conditions to cope with.

But it's now, in the job you have, under the existing conditions, that you are being weighed. It is the way you cooperate with your co-workers that will affect your chances of advancement. It is the way you handle your first job that will decide whether you will get a better one. It is the efficiency with which you perform the simple, and often dull, tasks that will promote you to more complex jobs.

It's the little things, keeping cheerful and well-groomed and alert, being prompt and attentive and accurate, that lead to the bigger things. Fight against things as they are and you only will exhaust yourself, for you are unlikely to change them. Adjust yourself to them and you will learn that with a little tact and intelligence you can often change them for the better.

What do you want to make of your job? Before you answer quickly that you want to make good at it, stop and think twice. Are you sure that you do? Nearly anyone will be inclined to say that he is ambitious, but it isn't often the case. Very few people have real ambition. Most people are actually lazy.

True, they have that dream picture in their minds of all the glories attending their success, but they aren't doing anything about it, not if it requires any exertion.

Dreaming is a pleasant occupation—and easy! The only ambition such people have is to arrive at some state of comfort where they can be even lazier than they are now.

The really ambitious person is one who has an overwhelmingly strong desire to accomplish something and be somebody. Ambition, of course, may be of a low order or a high one: it may be frankly selfish or it may contain the elements of wanting to contribute something and be somebody.

Constructive ambition is one of the strongest motivating powers you can possess. All constructive ambition is founded on ideals—of service, of accomplishment—as well as on the ideals which you have in mind for yourself. A person of low ideals is not apt to be of much value and a person of no ideals at all is very often lacking in any plan or ambition. The worthwhile person has clear ideals, the ambition to work for them, and is constantly building and perfecting plans to accomplish his or her purpose.

That phrase "constructive ambition" indicates a whole lot more than wishful thinking. Offices and plants and factories and stores are overrun with people who wish they had better jobs, who are convinced they could do as well as Tom if they had a chance at his job, or who think what a fine job they could do if all the conditions were different. Many of these people believe that this vague desire for something better is ambition.

Constructive ambition doesn't waste energy in wishful thinking. It doesn't avoid the issue by hiding behind the phrase "if things were different". It takes things as they are and finds a way of using them as they are. It plans a way of making the next step in advance instead of dreaming pleasantly that the step has been made.

Naturally, ambition in itself isn't enough. It takes

perseverance to achieve your ambition; it takes steadfastness and long-continued application; it takes determination, diligence, and patience. All these words have been drummed into you so much, you have heard them so often, that you turn away from them in impatience, muttering that they are hackneyed, platitudinous, the same old thing. Unhappily that is true. Most of the basic truths are ancient indeed. There's nothing new in plain common sense, for that matter. Yet each generation has to learn for itself that these things are true.

It's your life and your job. What are you going to do with them? Wait for someone else to tell you what to do? Complain because things aren't constructed after your heart's desire? Retire into a dream world where everything's rosy? Or roll up your sleeves and tackle the problem with all the energy you have?

The Right Boss—
or The Wrong One

Once you have analyzed your own aptitudes and discovered where they will fit in best, you have considerably narrowed the field in which you are going to work. Now look around the field you have selected and if it is humanly possible for you to do so, choose your boss. The *right* boss. On him depends, far more than the inspiration books would suggest, the opportunity to do your best work and to get the most from it.

But unless you have chosen an enlightened boss who recognizes the importance of rewarding good service and advances his employees according to their merit and their value to his business, you are wasting your time. In other words, if you have the right attitude, your superiors should have the same attitude toward you. Do not work for a man who merely tries to exploit you. If you are wise you will try, if possible, to avoid exploiters and to work for people who are unselfish enough to be interested in your progress. The most fortunate people in business are those who have an opportunity to do this.

Andrew Carnegie, when asked on one occasion

whether he was not worried for fear some of the young men he was training would take his place, shook his head and replied, "All that worries me is that they won't."

By all means, sacrifice anything within reason to work under a good boss. I have seen many employees so eager to make just a little more money that they have foolishly left sympathetic and able employers to work for others who were not. It isn't, of course, necessary to work for starvation wages in order to take advantage of such an opportunity. As a matter of fact, the reverse is generally true. Such people are more apt to pay higher wages than the other type, simply because they are generally more able and run their businesses more efficiently.

I hear a chorus of voices saying that the choice is not in their hands, that jobs are few and hard to get, that they can't afford to wait until they find the ideal employer or the ideal company. Or if they acknowledge that their chief is not a man who is likely to advance them or to take an interest in their welfare, they can't give up their jobs for the reason that they don't like their boss.

Of course, I realize that it is not often possible to leave your job if you find your employer is not an enlightened person. Jobs are hard to get and you must earn a living and you cannot always choose. But it is important to remember that it is difficult to do a constructive piece of work unless you are doing it for a constructive chief.

How are you going to recognize the employer who will take an interest in your welfare and advancement? That is not difficult. Is there frequent turn-over of personnel in his company? Are his employees keen about their work and hopeful of their prospects for the future, or do they go around with a discouraged air, the atmosphere of a continual Blue Monday about them, as though their jobs were like sentences to a chain gang, hanging on simply because they can't find anything better?

If your employer is an able man, his knowledge of you and interest in you does not end when he has summed up your aptitudes and capabilities and assigned you to a job. He continues to watch you, to observe your work, to check up on the qualities you display which indicate your fitness for what you are doing.

If you have the right boss, he is a man who realizes that it is good for his business to advance you when you have displayed competence and ability, to move you ahead into positions of greater responsibility where his company can get the benefit of all you are capable of, rather than merely a fraction of it.

With the right type of a boss there is no danger of being lost, of becoming an anonymous cog in a big machine. Such people have recognized the fact that their man power is as important as their products, that a stock inventory twice a year is no more essential than a personnel inventory every six months. They know what their people are doing, how they are handling their work, where they have given indications of unusual ability, where they have made mistakes. They make a point of talking these things over with the employees themselves, discussing their good and bad points frankly with them.

Any employee who has worked for the right kind of boss can tell you the advantages of this type of check up. It removes the tension and uncertainty in which too many employees live because they don't know where they stand, how their superiors feel about them, or whether they are even aware of them. They have the security which comes of knowing that what they do is weighed justly and fairly.

The company which makes no periodic check up of the

work of its employees is probably indifferent to them. While the poor worker may not be observed, the good worker runs the risk of being disregarded too, and receiving no proper reward for his efforts. The boss who keeps an eye on you is trying to help you as well as to develop a more efficient staff.

The right boss believes that the dignity of the employee must be respected. Companies with good managements are constantly on the alert to see that straw bosses do not take advantage of their positions, that they are not unfair to those under them, that they are not permitted to adopt a dictatorial air. Minor executives are the cause of much labor trouble today, and the right company takes care that the old time "overseer" attitude is not allowed to make the lives of employees miserable.

In general, in all industries, working conditions have been improved, and most companies today have reasonable hours, a healthful amount of light and air, proper rest rooms, and so forth. But the important thing is good management. When the policies of a company are not clear, there is an air of confusion and employees are floundering because they do not know what their objectives should be. There is no gain in working for such companies, either in the experience you will get or in promotion. And you will find that it is not easy to sell your services to other companies after working too long for such a concern because the work you have done will not be highly regarded elsewhere.

Almost everyone is familiar with the dreadful blunders which result from bosses who lack judgement. This ability is found in varying degrees, and the more advanced the work, the more necessary good judgement is. Many have been promoted to positions which require greater judgement than they possessed and their ultimate failures were tragic. Someone once said that a good executive must make four good decisions, five fair ones, and only one really bad one, out of ten. The man who advances you if you lack this quality (of good judgement) is himself showing bad judgement for which his business will have to pay a heavy toll.

Every swing of the business pendulum catches men who have planned badly because of lack of foresight. It is easy to see evidences of an employer's failure to look ahead and to plan. The greater the responsibility in business, the more necessary it is to plan ahead, and there are not very many men with this ability. So you see it is to your own advantage to try to determine whether the executive who employs you is planning soundly. If he does not, you are one of those who will suffer.

If your superior is worth working for, he will be a man of courage: not foolhardy courage, but real courage, governed by intelligence and character. Not the kind that plunges blindly ahead, regardless of consequences, but the kind that weighs carefully before he proceeds, taking no unnecessary chances, but not hesitating when chances must be taken.

It can easily be understood, of course, that any man who is in charge of thousands of employees must never permit himself to jeopardize their jobs or their well-being by taking hazardous chances which are not carefully and intelligently considered. Conversely, he must have the courage to take necessary action which, in the long run, will be beneficial to all concerned. The ultra-conservative man who takes no chances is the one you frequently meet in business today. He is neither foolhardy nor constructively courageous. You will generally find him in charge of businesses which are standing still or sliding into obscurity.

I recall the case of an executive of this type who managed a branch factory. The factory kept losing ground. Decisions were not made. Things drifted along in a way that interfered with the flow of work in other departments. The employees had no sense of security, no faith in his judgement, no confidence in the fact that things would get better. They were restless and discontented, and there were frequent labor troubles. Instead of embarking in a stout craft for a known destination, they felt as uncertain as though they were adrift in a rudderless boat. The executive had been left in charge because no other individual could be found in the company who had the experience to replace him.

The president of the company, however, after carefully considering all the factors, had the courage to place in charge of the factory a man who, although lacking in experience, had more than his share of intelligence and ability. During his first year of operation the plant suffered from his lack of experience, but at the end of that time, the output began to forge ahead and efficiency began to replace inefficiency.

After two years of operation, the courageous step was fully justified. Not only had the volume more than doubled, but the curve of expenses had gone down rapidly and, wonder of wonders, the average pay of the workers had also increased. Such intelligent courage is much needed in business and is a quality which the employer will expect to find in ambitious individuals. He himself must have the courage to break through obstacles, to fight for what he believes, and finally, by courageous perseverance, to achieve his ends.

Management has not progressed, except in a few isolated instances, to the point where it can utilize the capabilities of employees in the most intelligent way. It is my firm conviction that if we could rescramble all the people in American business today, putting them into the right spots, where they could do the work for which they are best fitted, there would be a tremendous improvement in business efficiency. But instead of this, we have a tragic waste of manpower, of frequently misdirected people struggling with jobs for which they are not equipped, while the talents and capabilities which would be of enormous value to the business world become atrophied from lack of productive use. Economic waste. Waste of ability. Waste of effort. Waste of human beings.

In spite of the fact that many people feel that spiritual values have no place in business, I am of the opinion that such contentions are old-fashioned and have outlived their day. Spiritual values are necessary for people in responsible positions, and are becoming increasingly recognized as being more important today than craftiness and cunning were in years past. If you have the right boss, he or she is endowed with these spiritual values.

Great leadership in business or elsewhere cannot exist without spiritual values. You will find that the person with a deep sense of ethical principles and high spiritual values will be more and more in demand as time goes on. For example, not long ago a company with which I was familiar inaugurated the practice of bestowing gold medals on those employees who had rendered the highest standards of distinguished service. It is interesting to note that among the standards used in choosing the recipients, spiritual values were high on the list.

What's Your Attitude?

Recently I attended a conference on vocational problems at a large Eastern university. I had been invited to speak on the subject of "After College, Business." As I circulated among the guests, I asked several of the students what they would like to have me tell them about business. Most of them said, "The thing that interests me most is how to get a job."

This attitude toward business on the part of many undergraduates does not seem to be either realistic or constructive. The emphasis was all on the get—get a job, get something. I met only a few whose attitude was, "I want to find a spot where I can be really useful."

One man, while discussing this subject with me, told me his ambition was to make a million dollars and retire. I explained to him that all he needed to do was to find a job that was suited to his talents. Then if he could bring in about one hundred million dollars' worth of business he would probably be paid a million dollars for his efforts. This was a great disappointment to him because he was anxious to make his million dollars without having to do the work which the hundred million dollars' worth of business seemed to call for.

The idea of making a pile and retiring, to live on some southern beach or other pleasant place seems to be held by certain types of people. In some way or another, they expect to make the money and quit. They want to make no effort, and above all, they do not intend to contribute a thing to others, but they never seem to doubt that they are entitled to something for themselves.

This idea of "Get what you can, as fast as you can, and as easily as you can," is nonsense. The slightest study of business, its functions and its operation, will show you that it is not practical. The most superficial scrutiny of the careers of men who have tried to get ahead on such a frivolous idea will show you that it is unworkable. Business is not a lottery nor a grab bag from which you snatch what you can, at as high a salary as possible; nor is it merely a springboard from which you leap to another position on the blind chance of a few dollars more.

There's one point that you will have to get straight. The men and women who make progress in business put in more than they take out—more effort, more time, more thought. The man who is not worth more than his salary, who is not giving more than he is paid to do, hasn't a chance to progress because he isn't being profitable to the company who hires him. That fact may be disillusioning, but it is common sense, and it applies all along the line, except if you work for the government. And the bigger the job, the more you must put into it in proportion to what you take out. That fact ought to be written into every primer so that people could learn it early in life. It would save a whole lot of misunderstanding later on. And it might cure a lot of people of looking on business as a sort of sweepstakes where, if you are lucky, you draw a winning number.

It is generally true that the highest paid men in business are generally underpaid. I realize that it is hard for the person who earns between eight and twelve thousand dollars a year to feel that someone whose income is in the hundreds of thousands of dollars isn't being overpaid for what he does. Nevertheless, it is a fact that there is a larger percentage of men in the fifty thousand dollar and up class who are being underpaid for what they contribute, than there is in the eight to twelve thousand dollar group. One of the reasons for this is that these higher-paid individuals have the imagination and the capacity to build great organizations.

I believe one problem is that too many people have the idea that business exists in order to support those who have jobs in it. Nothing could be further from the truth. This is only a secondary objective. Business exists primarily to serve its customers. Any business that does not serve its customers well will go out of business. Don't think that all you have to do is to get a job and from then on business will support you. Business will never do that and no laws made by any governing body, state or national, can accomplish it.

Don't misunderstand me. I am not advocating that you go into business just for altruistic reasons. Obviously, that would be a short-sighted notion. But neither do I advocate that you go into business purely and selfishly to make money for yourself and for no other reason. Instead, I would substitute the idea of intelligent selfishness, which means that in addition to getting something for yourself, you must also contribute something for others: for your customers, for your employees if you are an employer, for the stockholders, and for the community where your business is.

Preachments that business owes people a living will create nothing but chaos. This philosophy has reached people in colleges and schools, and it causes them to start in business with the most erroneous ideas.

If you are ambitious to succeed in business, make up your mind that your hours will be long and that you will work harder than you have anticipated; much harder I can assure you, than you ever did in school or college.

The Person Behind the Job

Behind every job there is a person, and behind the job which you have found is you. You took the job after a long search, after a process of elimination and experimentation, and you intend to make good at it. You have mastered the routine, you are working hard, you are getting along well.

What comes next? A lot of people will tell you that if you handle this job well you will be advanced another step, and so on, up the ladder. But these people are overlooking a significant thing. In preparing yourself to handle more responsibility, and to become a more important factor in your business, *you must develop as a person.* This is not simply a question of training, or of education, or of acquiring more and more information about your job. It is a question of reaching beyond the boundaries of your job, of widening your personal horizon, of becoming broader, richer, more significant as a human being.

"He isn't big enough for the job," executives frequently say in passing over one man and advancing another. What do they mean? Not that his efficiency is not up to standard, not that he lacks knowledge about his particular job, but that the man, as a person, is small, his horizon is limited, his comprehension of other people is shallow, his spiritual values are meager—his whole makeup is on a petty scale.

It is the rarest thing in the world for people to develop all their potentialities. *It is my conviction that one of the greatest crimes a person can commit is to waste himself by developing only part of his capacities.*

This is not a book on how to be successful. It is designed merely to tell you some common sense facts about business as it is practiced today and about some of the methods which will help you to find the place in it where you can do the best work and, as a result, lead a reasonably satisfactory life. But the thought of success was probably in your mind when you picked up this book; perhaps you even entertained the dim hope that at last someone had discovered the secret that points the way to the pot of gold at the end of the rainbow.

I do not subscribe to the popular conception of success in business, which is, that the person who makes the most money is the greatest success. This idea makes for widespread unhappiness. Those who do not achieve money success feel that they have been failures and often do not even try to find other outlets for their energies. They become permeated with a sense of frustration which robs them of much of their essential usefulness.

Is success, then, only for the few? Under that definition it is, but it shouldn't be. Any person can be successful. What is success? It is the utilization of all your capacities to the full. That is why I emphasize developing yourself as a person. Of course, it will have a direct bearing on your career, but over and above that, it will enlarge your understanding, enrich your life, and give it a significance which you cannot attain in any other way.

When businesses get into difficulties, it is often discovered that the man at the head of the company during the time when it was going downhill was someone whose horizons had never grown, someone whose sense of values and comprehension of the broad, human equations were dwarfed or undeveloped. In other words, he was a small person and should never have been put in the position of managing thousands of people. In my opinion, part of the discontent found in industry today is due to the fact that some of the leaders of industry have been narrow and small-gauged people.

How can you develop into a bigger person? First, I'd like to point out how not to develop: limit your energies and your interests to doing your job, nothing but your job. Suppose, for instance, that you are a reporter on a newspaper. By doing your assignments promptly and well, by filling in spare time in reading newspapers, you may become a skilled reporter. But nothing more. Your job is a groove in which you are standing. Entrench yourself in it, exclude every interest which has no bearing on your particular problems, and that groove will deepen and become a rut in which you will have mentally sunk. Widen your groove, look around you!

The reporter who limits himself to covering his assignments remains a reporter. But suppose he looks beyond his own job, interests himself in the policies of his newspaper, informs himself about the aims of the management. Suppose that instead of confining himself to his narrow routine, he learns to think broadly and understandingly about the policies his paper advocates, about the situations he encounters in the course of his work.

His work offers a tremendous opportunity to learn by investigating sidelines pertaining to his assignments.

I know a newspaper man who, years ago, started work as a reporter. He devoted his evenings to studying typography and became keenly interested in the history of printing. Years later he wrote an important article on the invention of moveable type by Gutenberg. From an authoritative knowledge of printing, he went on to the study of type faces, and as a result, he was able to make some important suggestions to a prominent catalog publisher. He was so highly commended to his own superior for this that it resulted in a substantial advance for him.

You see, there is an unfortunate trend today toward too much gathering of information, too much of what is known as training, and not enough of those broadening interests which will develop you as a person.

One of the most delightful men I know is a gardener by trade. But he can discuss painting and art, and spends most of his free time in museums, absorbing color, arrangement, and composition. Not only does his employer enjoy him as a person, but his artistic knowledge is reflected in his arrangement of flowers and in the planning of his garden. This is very different from being a run-of-the-mill gardener, different not only in the quality of work he does, but in the enrichment of his own mind. He not only makes his gardens beautiful for others, but also he has made his own life significant, by enlarging his knowledge, expanding his field of interest, getting a keener zest out of living.

Don't raise the objection that a variety of interests is implicit in the reporter's job, and the creation of beauty in that of the gardener, but that nothing can be done with your own dull job. Remember that I pointed out earlier the essential thing is to extend your interests beyond your job.

A friend of mine told me that she always went to a certain hairdresser, although the trip was an inconvenient one for her. But the hairdresser was interested in philosophy and could discuss it entertainingly and informatively while working on her hair.

A waitress in a restaurant devoted her free time to music, learning to know the great composers, to listen to music intelligently, to understand the structure of symphonies. Her recognition of the music in a score led a diner to take an interest in her, and talk to her, and slowly drew more and more musicians to her tables. When the slack season arrived and other waitresses were laid off, she remained on the job, because people remembered her and returned to her. A waitress may be excellent in her work and remain an automaton. This one made herself a person.

An able salesman of my acquaintance saved his money and took a trip to Europe. In some respects, it was one of the most significant things he ever did because it developed him tremendously. He had planned his trip because he wanted to get the most out of it, to see all he could, and to understand what he saw. He went to the places where the things he sold came from—Rome, Paris, Berlin, Brussels—and they became actualities to him instead of names on a map. True, it was invaluable to his job, not only because he could speak more intelligently and with authority, but also because his interest in his merchandise and its background made him more convincing than he had ever been before in his life. But it did more than that—it opened new fields of interest which stimulated his mind and broadened the groove in which he moved.

There is a delightful older woman who is a salesclerk in a department store. Efficient as she is at her work, she has not limited herself to it. Instead, she has read widely in American history with which she is as familiar as many professors. Because of the range of her interests, she has not only made herself unusually interesting to talk with, so that the wives of former presidents of the United States insist on her waiting on them whenever they are in the store because they like to chat with her, not only about history, but to discuss informal anecdotes which she has picked up from others who have played important roles on the political scene. Her groove is not limited by a counter in a store. It is wide enough to take in the whole panorama of American history.

One woman of my acquaintance interested herself in psychology, which not only stood her in good stead in bringing up her children, but later, when her husband died, leaving her practically destitute, she was equipped to join a bureau for vocational guidance where her understanding of psychology helped her in advising young people.

One of the best secretaries I ever saw was not satisfied with training herself to take notes rapidly and to transcribe them without all the annoying mistakes that sometimes occur. She studied her employer's personality, and before long he required only a few words to indicate what he wanted to say; she was able to write his letters just as he would have dictated them, and often, indeed, much better.

Measure the groove you live in. Has it changed in the past three years? Is it broader or narrower than it was then? How many new interests have you acquired in that length of time? We all know people whose groove is as narrow as a knife edge. They have plotted out their course, everything is cut and dried, and they go on in the same way, day after day, year after year, doing the same things, meeting the same people, thinking the same thoughts, making their lives a sort of dreary treadmill. And they are pretty dull people to know.

The flat person is not apt to be sought out by his friends. They already are as familiar as he is with his ideas, his opinions, and the dull routine of his life. The automobile man who can discuss nothing but cylinders, the man who comes to dinner and recites statistics because he has nothing else to contribute to the conversation, the person who knows only his own business, isn't much in demand. In fact, most of us run away from them. And that in itself is hampering. Because people are a part of our development, knowing people, understanding people, is an intrinsic part of broadening oneself as a person.

Go out of your way to meet people, not simply people of your own kind, people who share your own interests. The more types of people you know, the more viewpoints you can understand, the richer your life will be. You don't live in a vacuum you live in a world of people. Find out about them. The man who drives the taxicab, the boy who runs the elevator, have some ideas that it would be worth while listening to.

Of course, there is always that complaint of the half-hearted, that alibi of the insincere: there isn't time. Yes, I'd like to do these things if I had leisure. When I get home from work I like to sit around and rest. What are you waiting for? Are you thinking that when you are old and full of years and retired there will be ample time to use the abilities you've neglected all your life, time in which to make yourself more of a person? In God's name, use what you've got! It is of no use to you or to anyone to let your talents lie dormant, to let your abilities rust for lack of use. You might as well be dead as half-dead; and unused ability isn't a frozen asset, it's deadwood. And it makes you a bloody bore!

How do you spend your vacations—playing on a beach, camping in the mountains? Have you ever thought of using your vacation time creatively, planning it with an objective in mind? The usual vacation sends a person back to work more tired than when he started, and just about where he was in other ways. Why not use it as a springboard, not merely for exercising your physical muscles, but as a starting point for new interests. Travel is the ideal means of doing this: seeing historical places, meeting new people, and then following it up, on your return, by reading about the things you have seen, by using it as a stimulus to new studies. Travel in itself is valueless unless you bring to it a curiosity about the unknown, a desire to see and experience and comprehend new things. One young woman who had visited every country in the world remarked indifferently that she never went inside museums; she preferred to remain outside with the husbands and the umbrellas. Another young woman, who took her vacation creatively, planned her trips in advance and on her return read all that she could find about the places she had seen, so that her trip was not simply a matter of drifting from one place to another, but became a significant experience.

Travel does not need to be an elaborate affair of visiting foreign countries. How much do you know about your own city? A young man from a small southern city went to New York to spend a summer studying slum conditions. When he returned and related his experiences, a cousin of his, who was a social worker, laughed and said: "Come with me tomorrow, and let me show you your own town. You don't know anything about conditions here, you don't know how people live, you've never looked beyond the comfortable neighborhoods where your friends live."

One way to discover unknown aspects of your own community is to engage in some charitable work. Learning to grasp the problems of other people, learning to win their confidence, will help you to broaden your groove, help you to be a richer person.

What are you learning on the side? You should be studying something which has nothing to do with your job. But I want to make it clear that the object of such study should be to broaden you, your interests, your sympathies, your knowledge. It should have nothing to do with those glittering promises which are held out to people today, promises to make them writers or artists, actors or musicians, beautiful or charming, in ten easy lessons in their spare time. It is the will-o'-the-wisp of those ten easy lessons which has led thousands of people who ought to know better to believe that a book or a lecture or a bit of abracadabra will turn them into someone else, or will endow them with the qualities they lack. Common sense should tell them that, if the secret of beauty and charm and talent were so simple, the world would have discovered it long ago; that all of us, in the natural course of events, would have become beautiful, charming, and talented. It would be nice, of course, if it were true. The only trouble is, it is not.

A prominent banker in New York studied the making of furniture in his spare time. It was a complete change from his business, it gave him an opportunity to make things with his own hands, and taught him a great deal. As a result, he acquired a deeper appreciation of artistic, inventive people and got greater enjoyment out of meeting them. The broadening of his interests also made him a more sympathetic person.

Two or three times a month a little group of some twenty Cleveland men meet in the evenings, set up their easels, and begin to paint. Some of them are doctors, some lawyers, bankers, businessmen. But they have one thing in common. They all want to paint. None of them has made a career of art. None of them is under the slightest compulsion to attend the meetings. They paint because they like it. Their work may not be important, it may not be handed down for awed generations to gaze at, but they are expressing instead of stifling a creative urge. They are developing a sense of perspective, a keener apperception, an awareness of color.

One of them pointed out a big skyscraper to me. "I used to think it was gray, " he said; "I hadn't learned how to see color. But it is a mass of colors—nearly twenty-four of them."

Too many of us look at gray buildings all of our lives when we might see them glorious with color. Why go through life blind?

The more you see, the more you hear, the more you experience, the more of a person, you will become. You need not be satisfied with a gray world. Why should you?

First in the big cities and later throughout the country, the amateur musician is coming into his own. Television and radio, instead of extinguishing him altogether as some people prophesied, have merely stimulated his urge to create his own music. Amateur orchestras, amateur string quartets, are struggling along, learning harmony and counterpoint, becoming more familiar with great music than they could by merely listening. They may never prove serious rivals of professional musicians, but they are making music an intrinsic part of their lives.

81

One of the best ways of enlarging your horizon is by selective reading. *Make a plan for yourself.* Choose a subject that interests you and then work out a course of reading and devote an hour a day to it. One young man found after getting out of college that he hadn't time to read, so he used to get up at six-thirty every morning and did an hour's reading before breakfast. After all, Anthony Trollope held a government position for many years, and yet he managed to write an incredibly large number of books, nearly all of them written in the early morning before breakfast.

But if you want to accomplish anything by your reading, don't leave it to chance, don't be haphazard about it, don't pick up any book that comes along. Make your plan and then stick to it. If, at the end of a period, you want to choose another subject, do so, but use the same general system.

Frederick the Great, if you will recall, did not content himself with just being a great military leader. He was wise enough to know that a man's interests must reach out as widely as possible. He requested Voltaire to visit him so that Voltaire might teach him to write poetry and discuss philosophy. He even learned to play a musical instrument well and to compose music.

The unhappy Louis the Sixteenth was a locksmith—and a very good one. The French statesman Herriot became interested in the life of Madame Recamier and wrote the best biography of her. Einstein, probably the world's most distinguished scientist, was an amateur violinist of great skill. Heifetz, the great violinist, collected rare books.

You don't want people to say: "He's not big enough for the job." "He has made no effort to widen the groove in which he lives." For, if you are to be given more responsibility, if you are expected to solve things others cannot solve, you must have more equipment. It isn't enough to be skilled in your job. It isn't enough to have knowledge of your one little corner. You must be able to see out around the surrounding territory, and to understand what you see. There must be a real person, a fine human being behind your job.

About the Author

Mr. Walter Hoving is chairman of the board of Tiffany & Co.

He is a graduate of Brown University and was formerly a vice president of R. H. Macy & Co., vice president of Montgomery Ward, president of Lord & Taylor, and president of Bonwit Teller. While head of Lord & Taylor, Mr. Hoving initiated the Lord & Taylor American Design Awards to encourage original design in this country.

He is a past president of the Fifth Avenue Association, the National Institute of Social Sciences, the Commerce and Industry Association of New York, and a former trustee of Brown University.

Mr. Hoving received the Michael Friedsam Medal and honorary doctorates from Brown University, (LL.D.), Long Island University, (L.H.D.), and Pratt Institute, (LL.D.).

In 1973 Mr. Hoving sponsored The Tiffany Lecture Series on Corporate Design Management at The Wharton School at The University of Pennsylvania. The purpose of the lectures was to expose the students to the importance of esthetics in the many facets of business management. These lectures were subsequently published in a book, *The Art of Design Management.*

He is also the author of *The Distribution Revolution,* and *Tiffany's Tablemanners For Teenagers.*

Mr. Hoving is the founder of the Salvation Army Association of New York and served as its president for twenty years. He helped found the United Negro College Fund, the U.S.O. and was chairman of the U.S.O. National Board during the Second World War.